CHONDA

UNASHAMED

A **BIBLE STUDY** ON **SHAME**
AND **BEING UNASHAMED**

FOR **WOMEN'S SMALL GROUP**
OR **PERSONAL STUDY**

BY **CHONDA PIERCE** AND **MIKE COURTNEY**

For those who want to live boldly for Jesus. You've got this!

Edited by Pamela White

Table of Contents

About the Authors

Chonda Pierce

Drawing on both the craziness and the pain of her Southern upbringing, Chonda Pierce has been entertaining audiences from coast to coast for more than 20 years. She tells stories, funny stories, then opens her soul unashamedly to expose the pain and heartbreaks of her life. That rare combination of humor and honesty has opened doors in nearly every media platform.

Chonda has authored eight books, has ranked among Pollstar's top-selling live performers, and has received an award from the RIAA as the best-selling female comedian in history.

She is very often a guest on the Grand Ole Opry, has served as host of the Christian Music Hall of Fame Awards and the Inspirational Country Music Awards, and has co-hosted the GMA Dove Awards. Chonda received five Daytime Emmy nominations for her work co-hosting *Aspiring Women*, and her first television special, "This Ain't Prettyville," appeared on CMT nationwide. She is a frequent talk show guest, appearing on *Life Today*, *The Wanda Sykes Show*, *The Mike Huckabee Show*, as well as ABC's popular talk show *The View*. She has been featured in numerous Hallmark Movies. Her movie *Unashamed*, the backdrop for this study, was her third mainstream theater movie.

Mike Courtney

Dr. Mike Courtney is a gifted writer, speaker, and counselor with 25 years of experience as a highly successful pastor. He is also a recovering addict who lives a 12-step life one day at a time. Mike is the director of Branches Counseling Centers, a group of nonprofit counseling centers in Tennessee and Florida that specializes in recovery from unwanted sexual behavior and couples in crisis. Branches utilizes the skills of both state licensed therapists and pastoral counselors, and the center never turns anyone away because of an inability to pay. From that platform, Mike tells his story of honesty, hope, and healing to audiences across America. He is the author of two books: *Failure and How I Achieved It* and *The John Book*. Oh, yes, he is also Chonda's brother.

The Value of Personal Bible Study

This is a collaboration. My brother, Mike, and I have a very normal family dynamic. He's a typical big brother. (Don't tell him I said that!) He worries about me finding a "real" job and rolls his eyes when I talk about my new dating life. As we decided to do this study together, he was quick to say, "I will focus on the coherent. You do the comical." He tried to write his parts in my voice because, he said, "Your voice is what people have come to love. Besides, it's loud. Really loud." And that's when I, as the little sister, get to roll my eyes right back.

We have a few things in common. At the top of that list is not just a love for God's Word, but the understanding that Bible Study is an absolute *must* in our lives. The world is on a fast pace, and if you're like me, you have become accustomed to moving quickly through most things. Yes, I actually stand and roll my fingers across the counter in my kitchen because the microwave popcorn is taking much too long. Let's be honest: we live, as never before, in an instant age. I hardly ever watch the news anymore. I can Google the headlines, breeze through the big stuff, read a few stories that are of real interest to me, and BAM, in six minutes I have done what it takes the nightly news guys an hour to do. I ask Siri to look up a word for me, Mr. Keurig makes my coffee, and Alexa tells me my weather and the weather around the world in an instant. Everything comes to me fast with very little effort on my part.

Why, then, should I set aside 20 or 30 minutes each day to get quiet, read (who does that anymore?), and work through some questions that I could probably find in a FAQ page on some website? Well, because of everything we just said above. While we live in an instant age, our hearts, our heads, and our souls were never made for that. We were created for quiet times, slow processes, deep reflection. Even in the original Garden, God came and walked with Adam and Eve in the cool of the day. We were made for communion. All of this fast, immediate, instant is short-circuiting our hardwire and destroying our ability to connect on an intimate level with the words on the page that perhaps God is wanting us to see, hear, taste, and touch.

Do you remember 1 John 1:1? "That which was from the beginning, which we have heard, which we have seen with our eyes, which we have looked at and our hands have touched—this we proclaim concerning the Word of life." John says, "There is more to this than just a quick fix. We should take the time to touch it, taste it, look deep into the roots of it, and then proclaim *that*." This personal Bible study is an invitation to do just that.

So, we invite you to set aside 30 minutes each day for six weeks to read, reflect, write, and meditate in order to touch and taste what God is trying to say. I promise you that we have written nothing so profound here that it will change your life. But I also promise you that if you give Him a chance, God will say something to you that will. It doesn't happen in an instant. It takes a little quiet space. It takes some work. It takes, ugh, I hate to say it, discipline.

Here's the plan. Designate a time each day. Try to stick with the same time. You may have to get up 30 minutes early. You may have to watch 30 minutes less of *Hawaii Five-0*. Set aside the same time each day for study and if you can, make your own space—a prayer closet, a favorite chair, an old recliner.

Mike has a designated space devoted to study in his house. He writes, "I have a couch in my home office where the lighting is good. I've got markers and my favorite Bible on the table beside me. I have a blanket to drape over my knees. I've got a coaster for my coffee cup (my wife's idea). About the only thing I do in that spot is Bible study, personal devotions. Doris, my wife, has a chair in the family room. Nice view out the window. Stack of books on the floor. Heavier blanket. Same coaster. That's her spot. There is something about that designated spot that when I go there my brain and my body says, 'We are going to do Bible study now. Let's put the other stuff on the back burner.' Develop the habit of a consistent time and a consistent place."

I meet God sitting on my comfy corner on my patio. The breeze flows through me while ten floors below the Cumberland River winds through the hillside filled with trees and cliffs. The view is breathtaking, even in the rain. I sit as my jam box plays my favorite playlists—everything from Kirk Franklin, Marvin Sapp or Tamala Mann to Zach Williams, Karyn Williams, Mercy Me, or The Martins. They prepare my heart to touch base with Jesus before I start my day. Yes, I meet God there every morning. Well, except when it's 30 or below; then, God meets me inside on the couch under my favorite quilt!

Start the habit. Most psychologists will tell you it only takes three or four weeks to develop a new habit. We picked six weeks, partly because that's all the writing we wanted to do. We hope the next six weeks will press this new habit into your life. You see, we believe when we stop the commotion, commit to the time, something miraculous happens. You build a relationship. God wants to break into your fast-paced, instant world and love on you in a way that you cannot imagine. We pray that God will begin to connect with you and you with Him in such a way that this becomes a habit you just can't live without. Habit becomes relationship and relationship becomes so infectious that you simply have to tell someone. Which brings us to the last point.

How to Have a Healthy Group

(From Mike)

Forty years ago, I was a young pastor on the staff of a great church in Mt. Vernon, Ohio. I was fresh out of school, knew it all, and was ready to be *unashamed* and to change my world. The first Sunday at this church the young college baseball coach came up to me and said, "Hey, let's meet for breakfast at five this Tuesday." I learned two things that first week, well, actually three. On a very unimportant side note, I learned there were two five o'clocks in one day. The two important things I learned were that I did not know as much as I thought I did and that I needed to have a small

10

group of people around me to speak into my life on a regular basis. That was forty years ago, and there has hardly been a season in my life since then that I have not met with a group of men. Currently, it's Thursday mornings at six. (I am not as spiritual as I was back then.) This group of guys has been meeting with me for twelve years. Usually it's about ten of us, which is a little too big, but we've been meeting long enough that we make it work.

Here's what I believe about healthy groups. First, we need them. We were made for communion (remember the last section), but we were also made for community. We really do need each other. There is something about the comradery and connection of a few close faith partners that clarifies the voice of God for me like nothing else. My guys have one eye fixed on heaven and the other eye focused on me. They can tell when things are a little off, when my vocabulary is getting too salty, or when I am getting bitter instead of better. And they will call me on it. I need that. Small groups were really what the early church was. Shoot, even Jesus started a small group. We need that fellowship in our lives if we are going to live *unashamed*.

The second thing about healthy groups is that we are not all at the same place, and that's okay. There are guys in my group who have been in the Way for fifty years. There are other guys who are just in the way. We all ebb and flow in our walk with Jesus. Sometimes, I am on the mountain, doing good, fired up, close. Other seasons I am fighting to keep my head above water and not throw in the towel. That's the value of the group. They help me when I'm struggling. I help them when they are. Three things we don't do: we don't panic, we don't judge, and we don't fix. We understand this is just a season for this guy. He's going to be okay. We don't get our panties in a wad. (Well, actually, that would be another group.) We don't condemn him or preach to him. We just sit with him and watch God work in his life.

Third thing, we don't all have the same number of words, but we all have a lot. Some people talk more than others. (Did I mention that Chonda is my sister?) That's okay, but we all need to talk. Those of us with many words try to be careful and not use all of them every time we meet. We try to make space for the few-word guys to put their two cents in. Sometimes, we have to pull that out of them: "Robert, what did you think about this verse?" Sometimes, we have to be willing just to sit in silence. But I can tell you every time the few-word guys talk, it's good. From the very beginning, remind yourself that the group is for you but is not about you. Listen for what God has to say to you in the words of your few-word friends.

Two final, very practical things about healthy groups. What happens in Vegas stays in Vegas. The value of the group is safety. It is a place I can open up, complain about my wife (not that I ever do that, of course), and know that everything we say here, stays here. Nothing will kill your group faster than a breach of trust.

Last, start on time and *end on time*. Remember the many-word guys? We don't like this rule, but short of a real breakout of the Holy Spirit—and that does happen in our group—we are committed to ending on time. We meet for one hour, and then most of us go to breakfast afterwards to continue the conversation and the fellowship. I would suggest you begin with no more than ninety minutes. Don't wear yourselves out.

This little study was written with the personal Bible study *and* the group time in mind. If you don't do the study, you won't have anything to say in the group. If you don't do the group, you will miss most of what God has to say. There are about seven key segments we suggest for the group time. They should be fairly easily done in ninety minutes. These are only suggestions. As your group gels, you will find your own ways of connecting and communicating.

Always remember that the purpose of the group is the group. Fellowship, fun, talking, praying together, praying for each other—all take precedence over anything that is written here. My prayer is that your group will live long after the Bible study is done.

Here are the seven segments with a brief explanation:

Prayer: Open each meeting with prayer. Perhaps, ask a different person to open each week. I'd suggest a group of six people that meets for six weeks. Each person takes a week.

Connection: We've included some kind of little icebreaker moment each week. These are, of course, all optional. Often it is a clip from *Unashamed*.

Centering: This is the scripture time. Make sure that the Word of God stays at the center of what you do.

Discussion: Go over some of your answers from this week's study together. Make sure everyone has a chance to speak about the questions that were most meaningful to them.

Activity: One optional suggestion would be to spend five minutes reaffirming what God said during your time together.

Community: The best part of the group may be outside the group. If the group feels comfortable with this, pair up and talk together briefly about prayer needs. Commit to pray for your prayer partner this week.

Closing: This is a quick summary of this week and a chance to make sure everyone knows about next week. It might be you are meeting at a different house each week. That's good but make sure the directions are clear.

One final idea: Make your six-week study a seven-week event. Begin with a night to watch *Unashamed* together. Have popcorn, get acquainted, talk about the group. You could pass out the Bible study books then. Just begin with a fun, pre-six-week get-together. Above all, have a blast. Thanks for being *unashamed*.

Week 1: Shame
Personal Study: Genesis 3

It began, as many things did, in the Garden. You know the story. God made the world and He stepped back and said, "This is good." He flung stars into the sky, hung the moon on the other side of the ocean, set an alarm clock to wake the sun every day, and then said, "This is good." God made living things like ducks and dogs and daffodils. He made majestic golden eagles with wingspans wider than a car, and He made hummingbirds the size of spark plugs and with just as much energy. He carpeted the meadows with wildflowers and filled the forests with wild animals. He made trees and trout and turtledoves and then said, "This is good." Then, in a moment of godlike genius, because He's God and all His genius is godlike, God made human beings, man and woman, fit for each other, the crowning glory of all that God had done, and God stepped back and said, "This is good. This is *real* good."

Then one day the serpent slithered in and said to Eve, the woman, "You are not good. You are not good enough. You should know more, be better, be smarter. You should be like God." So, Eve took the apple, she gave it to Adam, they took a bite, and KABOOM! Like a bomb dropping on Nagasaki, a mushroom cloud exploded across the centuries, all the way down to me and to you. Shame stabs into our hearts like a steel dagger. We look in the mirror every morning and say, "This is not good. I should be thinner. I should stand up straight. Maybe if I colored my hair or got a little tuck." And it goes far deeper than that. "What was I thinking? How could I have been so stupid? They can never forgive me. I can never forgive myself. I am an idiot. I am a fool. I am a mistake. I am so ashamed." We call that *shame*.

The movie *Unashamed* is about taking a stand when it costs something. It is about not being afraid to say, "This is what I believe" and "This is *who* I believe." But the hard part about being unashamed is that we have to overcome being ashamed. At the heart of our being ashamed is, well, shame. We are made by the world, by our parents, by the image we see in the mirror to feel less than, to feel not good enough, unable, unworthy. We breathe in shame like breathing in air. And when we are living in shame, we cannot be unashamed. So let's start here.

Isn't it interesting that the very first story in the Bible includes the introduction of shame? After the creation, shame has been with us as long as time itself.

In her movie *Unashamed*, Chonda bravely talks about her own shame. Watch the Bible study clip for chapter 1 found in the special features of the *Unashamed* DVD.

What does she say to you about shame that resonates with your story?

_____

Read Genesis 3:1-13 and let's talk about shame.

> Now the serpent was more crafty than any of
> the wild animals the LORD God had made. He
> said to the woman, "Did God really say, 'You
> must not eat from any tree in the garden'?"
> (Gen. 3:1)

Questions. Shame always begins with questions:
How could you? Why didn't you? What were you
thinking? When will you ever? In Genesis 3:1 the
serpent asked, "Did God really say, 'You must not
eat from any tree in the Garden'?" Most of the
enemy's questions have just a kernel of truth.

**What did God actually say, and how is that
different from what Satan accused Him of
saying?**

What half-truths has Satan been telling you about your life, story, or situation?

The lies didn't stop there.

> The woman said to the serpent, "We may eat fruit from the trees in the garden, but God did say, 'You must not eat fruit from the tree that is in the middle of the garden, and you must not touch it, or you will die.'"

> "You will not certainly die," the serpent said to the woman. "For God knows that when you eat from it your eyes will be opened, and you will be like God, knowing good and evil." (Gen. 3:2-5)

Look at the lie the serpent told. He said, "You will be like God." Read Genesis 1:26-27. They already were like God.

How does what Satan tells you compare with what God says about you?

Next, Adam and Eve learned what shame is.

> When the woman saw that the fruit of the tree was good for food and pleasing to the eye, and also desirable for gaining wisdom, she took some and ate it. She also gave some to her husband, who was with her, and he ate it. Then the eyes of both of them were opened, and they realized they were naked; so they sewed fig leaves together and made coverings for themselves."   (Gen. 3:6-7)

"And their eyes were opened." Shame is about seeing yourself with eyes unfiltered by the amazing grace of God. Frankly, we should all be ashamed, and we would if it were not for God's mercy and miracle in us.

Tell a story about seeing yourself with the grace of God. How did that produce shame in you before His grace and how did it relieve shame after grace?

After eating of the apple, Adam and Eve immediately sewed fig leaves together and tried to hide their shame.

How have you tried to hide your shame rather than allow God to remove it?

The worst was yet to come.

> Then the man and his wife heard the sound of the Lord God as he was walking in the garden in the cool of the day, and they hid from the Lord God among the trees of the garden. But the Lord God called to the man, "Where are you?" (Gen. 3:8-9)

Of all the tragedies that shame produces, the greatest tragedy is separation from God. Conviction encourages us to find God. Guilt will turn us to God. Shame causes us to hide from God.

How has shame separated you, or those you know, from God?

[Adam] answered, "I heard you in the garden, and I was afraid because I was naked; so I hid." And he said, "Who told you that you were naked? Have you eaten from the tree that I commanded you not to eat from?" The man said, "The woman you put here with me—she gave me some fruit from the tree, and I ate it." (Gen. 3:10-13)

To alleviate our shame, we look for some external cause, some reason outside ourselves. Shame always produces blame. My parents raised me wrong. My teacher messed me up. My boss is a jerk.

Why do you think we seek to blame others for our shame?

How does telling the truth help us overcome shame?

Conclusion

The story ends in judgment. Our sins do require judgment and God is indeed just, but His justice is couched in His mercy. Look at Genesis 3:21: "The Lord God made clothes from animal skins for the man and his wife and dressed them." After all of this, the God of the Universe stooped down in the very Garden that He had created and sewed animal skins together and made clothes for Adam and Eve. What has to happen in order to get a skin off an animal? Adam and Eve's sin brought death into the world for the first time." Think about that. God's heart must have been broken. All that He had put together, all that He had pronounced "This is good" over, had been destroyed in a moment. In one lie, one bite, the perfection that God put in place was perverted.

I remember when my son, Zach, was little he fell and cut his head, like all kids do. My husband, David, and I took him to the emergency room where he got a couple of stitches. I was terribly upset but even more astounded at how upset David was about Zach's potential scar. David said, "Now he won't be perfect."

God designed us to be perfect. Shame, introduced by the enemy, convinces us that we are not. Shame defiled everything that God desired for Adam and Eve. God is God. It would have been easy for Him to pull out His cosmic eraser, wipe the slate clean, and just start fresh. But God didn't do that. He made clothes for them. He threw a robe over the shoulders of Adam and Eve and said, "You do not need to be ashamed."

God never gives up. Never looks down. Never abandons. He has made a way out of our shame. Next week we will look at a story about that.

WEEK 1 Group Time

Prayer: Begin your group time with prayer. Pray for the Holy Spirit to give you courage to speak honestly, compassion to listen lovingly, and wisdom to respond tenderly.

Connection: Watch the video clip from *Unashamed* that you watched in your personal study. Talk for a while about the feelings that this clip stirs up in you.

Centering: Ask one person to read Genesis 3:1-13.

Discussion: Together, go over some of your answers from this week's study. Make sure everyone has a chance to speak about the questions that were most meaningful to them.

Activity: Have each person in the group draw a fig leaf on a blank piece of paper. In the middle of the fig leaf write the thing that you most often try to hide. Fold the paper up so that no one can see what you have written. (Save this paper until next week.) Pray as a group and ask God to remove the shame of that one issue from your life this week.

Community: If the group feels comfortable with this, pair up and talk together briefly about prayer needs. Commit to pray for your prayer partner this week.

Closing: Ask one person to read Genesis 3:20-24. Set the time and place for next week's meeting.

Week 2: And Peter
Personal Study: Mark 14 and 16

The Easter story addresses shame. Do you
remember the interesting little phrase the angel used
when he instructed the women in the Garden?
(That's right: we are back to a garden.) Look at
Mark 16 verse 7: "But go, tell His disciples and
Peter." It's that last little phrase that captures my
imagination. "Go tell His disciples *and Peter*." And
Peter. What in the world is that about? Well, think
about the story with me.

Let's go back to the upper room. Jesus was telling
His guys what was about to happen. He told them
that He was going to be betrayed. Peter opened his
big mouth (I'm just like Peter) and said, "Lord,
everybody else might turn tail and run, but not me,

Lord. Not me. You can count on me. I'll never betray you." I imagine Jesus just shook His head. Maybe He threw His arm over Peter's shoulder. He said, "I tell you the truth, Peter, today—yes, tonight—before the rooster crows twice, you yourself will disown Me three times" (Mark 14:30).

The story unfolded. Jesus was arrested. Peter grabbed a sword and cut off some guy's ear. Maybe Jesus was wrong. Surely, somebody as brave as Peter would not desert Him. They took Jesus away. Peter was milling around outside the courthouse. Some young girl said, "Hey, you're one of the disciples." It was a confusing moment. There was some panic. It was such a spur-of-the-moment thing. Peter said, "Nope. Not me. You have me mistaken with someone else. I don't know the guy." ERRRR! There it was. It happened. But look: It could have happened to anybody. Right place. Wrong time. Bad choice. We've all made that kind of blunder.

A moment later, a soldier said, "I think I saw you with Him." "No way," said Peter. "I'm not one of those fanatics." Another guy piped up, "Yea, I'm sure it was you." Peter cursed. "I told you I don't know Him. I've never laid eyes on Him. Just leave me alone." ERRRR! KABOOM! The mushroom cloud of shame swept over him like a punch in the gut. And Peter said, "Oh, my God. What was I thinking? I will never live this down. I am a failure. I'm no good. I am so ashamed."

Has there been a moment when a mistake, a failure, a world-class mess up has convinced you that God could never use you again? Tell about it.

Watch the Bible study clip for chapter 2 found in the special features on the *Unashamed* DVD of Chonda's interview with Danny Gokey. This is a story of someone who could have given up on God and stopped believing that he could be used for good. But he did not. Reflect on that.

Has there been a time when you thought God had given up on you? Talk about that.

Let's look at the story together.

> While Peter was below in the courtyard, one of the servant girls of the high priest came by. When she saw Peter warming himself, she looked closely at him. "You also were with that Nazarene, Jesus," she said. But he denied it. "I don't know or understand what you're talking about," he said, and went out into the entryway." (Mark 14:66-68)

Why is it so easy to deny Christ when the pressure is put on us by those who do not believe?

Shame. Shame is a horrible emotion to feel. It has got to be the one feeling that is manufactured entirely by the devil. Anger can be destructive, but it can also be righteous. Paul says, "Be angry but do not sin" (Eph. 4:26). Sadness is certainly a difficult feeling to live with, but sadness can be healthy in processing loss and dealing with grief. Pain is not fun, but most of the important lessons in life we learn come from pain. I like to say, "The only problem with pain is that it hurts." There are a lot of negative feelings and emotions, but they all have their necessary and positive sides. Except shame.

The story of Peter is a story of shame. He was overwhelmed by it, consumed with it. Can you imagine the thoughts running through his mind the very moment that he did the unthinkable, the one thing he swore he would never do?

> When the servant girl saw him there, she said again to those standing around, "This fellow is one of them." Again, he denied it. After a little while, those standing near said to Peter, "Surely you are one of them, for you are a Galilean." He began to call down curses, and he swore to them, "I don't know this man you're talking about." (Mark 14:69-71)

Shame will take us where we do not want to go and cause us to do things we never imagined.

Do you remember a time shame kept you from standing up for the Gospel or caused you to follow the crowd and do things you were not wanting to do? Are you willing to talk about it?

Shame is the one feeling that eats away at the root of our very being. Like a decayed tooth, it destroys any hope of being functional and does nothing but sit and hurt until it causes us to rot away. (Yuk, that's an unpleasant metaphor.) Shame, like no other feeling, works its way deeper and deeper into our souls until everything we believe about God, about others, and especially about ourselves is colored by shame.

Immediately the rooster crowed the second time. Then Peter remembered the words Jesus had spoken to him: "Before the rooster crows twice you will disown me three times." And he broke down and wept. (Mark 14:72)

Has shame brought you to your knees? Has shame driven you to tears? Has shame ever convinced you that God would never want to look at you again? Would you tell that story?

Shame is not guilt. Guilt is from God, I think. David said in Psalm 51, "My sin is ever before me, O God. Against You have I sinned." Guilt is about conviction. Shame is about condemnation. Guilt is about doing wrong. Shame is about being wrong.

Guilt is about what I have done. Shame is about who I am. Guilt, when addressed, makes me better. Shame, unless addressed, makes me more than bitter. Guilt says I made a mistake. Shame says I am a mistake. It causes me to loathe myself and lose any hope of reconciliation. Shame is awful, insidious, defeating, and destructive. It has to be from the devil.

But God is not, never has been, about shame. Guilt? When it is appropriate. Conviction? When it is necessary. But shame? Never. As a matter of fact, Hebrews 12:2 says that as Jesus was enduring the cross, He despised shame. A few days later He remembered Peter and the shame he was feeling. And He sent a message specifically to that guy who had failed so miserably.

> When the Sabbath was over, Mary Magdalene, Mary the mother of James, and Salome brought spices so that they might go to anoint Jesus' body. Very early on the first day of the week, just after sunrise, they were on their way to the tomb and they asked each other, "Who will roll the stone away from the entrance of the tomb?" But when they looked up, they saw that the stone, which was very large, had been rolled away. As they entered the tomb, they saw a young man dressed in a white robe sitting on the

right side, and they were alarmed. "Don't be alarmed," he said. "You are looking for Jesus the Nazarene, who was crucified. He has risen! He is not here. See the place where they laid Him. But go, tell His disciples and Peter, 'He is going ahead of you into Galilee. There you will see Him, just as He told you.'" (Mark 16:1-7)

Do you hear the redemption in that? Does it give you chills when the angel said, "and Peter"? This is the very heart of the Resurrection message. Jesus died and rose again to take away our shame.

Have you allowed Him to do that for you? Can you allow Him to? Will you? Write out verse 7 word for word, but in the place of Peter, put your name.

Now remember a time when Jesus took *your* shame away. Celebrate that here.

Conclusion

Jesus changed it all. He took all that shame away. He says to you right now, "Go tell Marilyn, go tell Sharon, go tell DeAnna, go tell Misty...."

That's what was going on with Peter. The angel said, "Go tell the disciples *and Peter*. Tell Peter he does not need to be ashamed. Tell Peter that Jesus loves him and took all this shame away. Tell Peter...." Tell Peter he doesn't have to be so bold and blustery. Tell him it's okay to be afraid sometimes. Tell him that he doesn't always have to have the answers, that "I don't know" is a perfectly acceptable response. Tell him that I love him just the way he is, without a mask. Nothing to prove and nothing to hide. No shame.

Here's what I want you to do, right now.

Acknowledge personal responsibility. The 12 Steps say, "We confessed the nature of our defect to God and one other human being." John says, "If we confess our sin, He is faithful and just to forgive us our sins and cleanse us from all unrighteousness" (1 John 1:9).

Accept and give full forgiveness. And accept His grace. Paul says, "Forgetting those things which are behind [my failures, my mistakes, my sins] and

41

reaching for what is ahead, I press on" (Phil. 3:13-14).

Alter the story you tell about yourself (inner healing prayer). In another place Paul says, "This means that anyone who belongs to Christ has become a new person. The old life is gone; a new life has begun" (2 Cor. 5:17).

I suggest to you today, don't be ashamed anymore. Take off your mask. Chase the alligator away. Confess right now that you have been wearing a mask for too long and accept His grace by praying a simple prayer: "Dear Jesus, You know me like no one else. And You love me like no one else. I take off my mask. I lay down my sin. I accept your forgiveness and grace. I can choose to stand confidently and joyfully because of You."

"Go tell my disciples and Peter…." He's talking to you, and He is telling you that you do not have to be ashamed. Next week, we will talk about *how* you do that.

Week 2 Group Time

Prayer: Begin your group time with prayer. Pray for God to remind you that He called you by name when He called you out of shame and into wonderful fellowship with Him.

Connection: Go around the group and have each person say one thing that they appreciate or admire about someone else in the group. Make sure that everyone is appreciated.

Centering: Ask one person to read Mark 16:1-7. When they get to the name "Peter," each person in the group shout out their own name there.

Discussion: Together, go over some of your answers from this week's study. Make sure everyone has a chance to speak about the questions that were most meaningful to them.

Activity: Read Revelation 2:17. Retrieve your fig leaf paper from last week. Open it up and redraw the fig leaf into a stone. (Or turn it over and start fresh.) Mark out the "shame" word from last week so that it cannot be read. On this stone write a new name for yourself, such as *Daughter*, *Chosen*, *Loved*, *Purchased*, or *Forgiven*.

Community: If the group feels comfortable with this, pick a new prayer partner for this week and talk together briefly about prayer needs. Commit to pray for your prayer partner this week.

Closing: Ask one person to pray. Set the time and place for next week's meeting.

Notes

Week 3: Overcoming
Personal Study: Revelation 12:7-11

Have you ever read a story that goes backwards and forwards at the same time? Like all of the Star Wars movies that started in the middle, moved to the future, then went back to the past. My husband, David, was a big Star Wars fan. He tried to take me with him a few times, but it didn't go well.

"Is this before Darth Vader or after Darth Vader?" I would whisper. (And you know how good I am at whispering.)

"This is Darth Vader before Luke Skywalker but after Darth Vader," he would answer.

"So, Luke Skywalker becomes Darth Vader?" with me whispering. "I don't know whether I'm coming or going."

"Why don't you go watch Toy Story in the next theater, Hon?"

An ancient story found in the last book of the New Testament is a lot like that. It goes way back before time began but stretches all the way into our lives today. I bring it up because it is the perfect place to go when we talk about shame. It is a story about both the beginning and the ending of shame. It is where we were before we even were and where we are going before we even get there. Let's read it together. It's found in Revelation, chapter 12. (Just go to the maps in your Bible and back up one book.)

> Then there was war in heaven. Michael and his angels fought against the dragon and his angels. And the dragon lost the battle, and he and his angels were forced out of heaven. This great dragon—the ancient serpent called the devil, or Satan, the one deceiving the whole world—was thrown down to the earth with all his angels.
>
> Then I heard a loud voice shouting across the heavens,
>
> "It has come at last—

salvation and power
and the Kingdom of our God,
and the authority of his Christ.
For the accuser of our brothers and sisters
has been thrown down to earth—
the one who accuses them
before our God day and night.
And they have defeated him by the blood of the Lamb
and by their testimony.
And they did not love their lives so much
that they were afraid to die." (Rev. 12:7-11)

The part that I want you to see is very near the end. "The accuser of the brothers and sisters has been thrown down to earth—the one who accuses them before our God day and night."

Let's start with the accuser. Sometimes, try as I might, I cannot get away from that voice in my head that calls me every name in the book and reminds me of every dumb thing I have done. Can I get a witness? I ask Alexa for my favorite praise music. I get my Beth Moore on. I even do a Tony Evans podcast, but there is still this message that won't go away that says, "I'm not good enough, I will never be loved, I should be ashamed of myself."

Have you ever gone through a season in your life when the voice of the accuser just refused to shut up? Write that story.

Revelation 12 says these accusations all began with a war.

> Then there was war in heaven. Michael and his angels fought against the dragon and his angels. And the dragon lost the battle, and he and his angels were forced out of heaven. This great dragon—the ancient serpent called the devil, or Satan, the one deceiving the whole world—was thrown down to the earth with all his angels." (Rev. 12:7)

I grew up in a church that was always talking about the battle for your heart. We sang songs like "Since Jesus came into my heart, since Jesus came into my heart" or "I've got the joy, joy, joy, joy down in my heart." We taught little kids to invite Jesus into their hearts. We warned teens not to go to movies because the devil would get in their hearts.

For the last ten or eleven years I have found myself fighting the same battle on a different battlefield, a battle not just for the heart but for the head as well. I am coming to see that the transforming work of the Holy Spirit to change man's heart is only a part of the story. God is also at work to change our heads. In fact, that may be the bigger war.

How does the "enemy" get in your head? What does he say to you? How does he make you think?

After the dragon—that's Satan—loses the war and is thrown out of heaven, he sets up camp on planet earth and the Bible calls him the accuser. Twenty-four hours a day, seven days a week, he sits on your shoulder and whispers shame words to you. "You're ugly. You're dumb. You're a hypocrite. You will never be enough." Maybe the voice in your head sounds like your mother. Maybe it sounds like a junior high teacher, an old pastor, a friend who betrayed you. If you are like me, most of the time the voice telling me how awful I am is my own voice.

What has the accuser been saying to you lately?

Now listen, I believe we give the old devil way too much credit. He is not nearly as powerful or as smart as we think he is. But he is an excellent historian and he has a super memory. He remembers and reminds you of every insult, every rejection, every mistake, every blunder you have ever made or endured or committed. He gets most of his ammunition from three places:

- Our parents: They may have meant well, but sometimes our moms and dads planted seeds in our heads that the accuser is still using against us today. "Don't eat that donut, honey, you know you have a tendency to be a little plump."
- Our past: Satan doesn't know everything, but he was there every time we messed up. I can't remember what I had for breakfast this morning but when the accuser starts talking to me, I can remember that shameful thing I did thirty years ago in living color.
- And our predicaments: The accuser tries to convince me that what is happening to me is a reflection of my worth. "If you really loved God, your kids would be in church today." Or, "If God really loved you, you wouldn't be fighting this disease right now."

Which one of these three things is the devil trying to use against you today? Explain that.

He wants to make us *think* we are purposeless, worthless, and hopeless. He fights the battle in our heads, and he tries to control our thinking. But we have seen the last Star Wars movie. (Or was it the first one?) We know how the story ends. WE WIN!

> They triumphed over him by the blood of the Lamb and by the word of their testimony. (Rev. 12:11)

Listen, the power of the accuser is broken in two ways. First by the blood of the Lamb. Jesus loved you so much that He shed His blood on the cross for you. Not some reluctant, just fulfilling-the-law kind of love. He really loves you. He is crazy about you. Take that, you old devil!

The second part of that verse says we overcome by the word of our testimony. We all have a God story. We remember it. We speak it. We testify to it and shout it from the mountain tops if we need to, proclaiming all the wonderful things that God has done for us. When Satan tries to accuse you and heap shame on you, start testifying to what God has done in your life.

Right now (on the following page) stop and make a list of fifteen ways God has blessed you in your life. I know you could write a thousand, but this is just a devotional workbook. We don't have that many pages.

1.

2.

3.

4.

5.

6.

7.

8.

9.

10.

11.

12.

13.

14.

15.

In 2 Corinthians Paul says, "For though we live in the world, we do not wage war as the world does. The weapons we fight with are not the weapons of the world. On the contrary, they have divine power to demolish strongholds. We demolish arguments and every pretension that sets itself up against the knowledge of God, and we take captive every thought to make it obedient to Christ" (2 Cor. 10:3-5). God has already provided everything we need to win this war against shame in our heads, but we have a part to play. We must be *intentional* about our thoughts. Joyce Meyer says, "We need to think about what we are thinking about."

Listen, you are not who Satan says you are. You are who God says you are. That's how we win the battle for our thoughts. We surrender our hearts to the Blood of the Lamb. We fill our minds with the Word of God. And we say we are who God says we are. We don't dwell on those negative accusations that Satan hurls against us. An old pastor friend of mine used to say, "You can't keep a bird from landing in your hair, but you don't have to let him build a nest."

Here's what do:

- Cover yourself with the blood of God.
- Immerse yourself in the Word of God.
- Talk to yourself with the voice of God.

Cover yourself with the blood of God. Take some time to write out your conversion story. Tell about the moment God saved you.

Immerse yourself in the Word of God. Begin to develop an arsenal of favorite Bible verses that you are ready to quote when Satan tries to play the blame game. Here are a few to get you started.

- "I have loved you with an everlasting love. I have drawn you with loving kindness" (Jer. 31:3).
- "What shall we say then in response to this? If God is for us, who can be against us?" (Rom. 8:31)
- "I can do everything through Him who gives me strength" (Phil. 4:13).

Write down five more "weapon" verses that you will memorize and use against the enemy.

1.

2.

3.

4.

5.

Finally, talk to yourself with the voice of God.
Call yourself right now what God calls you: *redeemed, forgiven, clean, powerful, loved, sober, free, accepted, beautiful.* Those are the words the

Lover of Your Soul has for you. Not that stuff the other guys says. Not that stuff your heard from your parents, in your past, or in your predicaments. Not the names you have been calling yourself. Start stopping those other words before they get started and use the Voice of God. When you hear another voice, even if it is yours, saying things that God would not say about you, stop it. Rebuke it. Go back to the Word of God. And then give yourself a good God talking to.

Right now, pray this, "God, tell me what you think about me." Now write it down.

Conclusion

In the movie *Kingdom of Heaven*, Orlando Bloom
(talk about a gift from God) is a knight during the
Crusades. He is trying to defend Jerusalem against
the Muslim army that seeks to overthrow it and kill
all the Christians inside. All of the other knights and
all of the soldiers have been killed. Balian (Orlando
Bloom) is left with just a handful of teenagers and
old men. The battle looks lost.

The priest comes to him and tells him to surrender.
The priest says, "How will you defend us? You
have no knights."

Balian turns to one of the teen boys in front of him
and commands, "Kneel." He says to all of the teens
and old men, "Every man capable of bearing arms,
kneel."

They kneel. He takes out his sword and lays it on
the shoulder of the first teen and recites the oath
that his father spoke over him. "Be without fear in
the face of your enemies. Be brave and upright that
God may love thee. Speak the truth always, even if
it leads to your death. Safeguard the helpless and do
no wrong—that is your oath."

Then he says to the teen and to them all, "Rise a
knight." It is an amazing scene. As they stand, you

see courage welling up in them. Their faces become stern, confident, brave.

The priest will have none of it. He says to Balian, "Who do you think you are? Do you think you can change the world? Does calling a man a knight make him a better fighter?"

Balian is walking away, but he turns and stares straight into the soul of the priest. In the most intense whisper you will ever hear, he says simply, "Yes!"

Does calling yourself a child of God help you overcome shame? Yes.

Does saying that Christ is at work in you make you a better fighter? Yes.

Does talking to yourself with the voice of God make you a stronger person? Yes. Yes. Yes.

You are not who Satan says you are. His accusations against you are not true. You are a deeply loved, totally forgiven, powerfully equipped child of the Most High God. Now, rise a knight, and never be ashamed again.

Next week we will look at a life that took that to heart.

Week 3: Group Time

Prayer: Begin your group time with prayer. Thank God for what He has done in and what He says about each one of you.

Connection: Watch the Bible study clip for chapter 3 found in the special features of the *Unashamed* DVD.

Centering: Ask one person to read Revelation 12:7-11.

Discussion: Together, go over some of your answers from this week's study. Make sure everyone has a chance to speak about the questions that were most meaningful to them.

Activity: Have every person write out one of their weapon verses on a card. Collect them. Read them out loud and try to guess who they belong to.

Community: If the group feels comfortable with this, pick a new prayer partner for this week and talk together briefly about prayer needs. Commit to pray for your prayer partner this week.

Closing: Rise a knight. Set the time and place for next week's meeting.

WEEK 4: Go Call Your Husband
Personal Study: John 4

The disciple John throws in little, seemingly random bits of information that later come back to change the whole tenor of the story: five loaves and two fishes; two more days: five thousand people. In a different story in John 14 about a woman and a well, it's time. John says, "It was about noon." Jesus and his entourage were passing through Samaria. That in itself is newsworthy. Most Jews would have gone way out of their way to *not* go through Samaria. They stopped at a little town called Sychar, and Jesus sat by the well while the disciples went to Arby's to get some roast beef sandwiches. (John also left out some important details.)

Let's read the story together.

> Now He had to go through Samaria. So He
> came to a town in Samaria called Sychar, near
> the plot of ground Jacob had given to his son
> Joseph. Jacob's well was there, and Jesus, tired
> as He was from the journey, sat down by the
> well. It was about noon.
>
> When a Samaritan woman came to draw water,
> Jesus said to her, "Will you give me a
> drink?" (His disciples had gone into the town to
> buy food.)
>
> The Samaritan woman said to Him, "You are a
> Jew and I am a Samaritan woman. How can you
> ask me for a drink?" (For Jews do not associate
> with Samaritans.)
>
> Jesus answered her, "If you knew the gift of
> God and who it is that asks you for a drink, you
> would have asked Him and He would have
> given you living water." (John 4:4-10)

While Jesus was sitting at the edge of town, a
woman came to the well and she and Jesus struck
up a conversation. John said it was about noon
(John 4:6). The conversation was about what you
would expect. Jesus asked for water. She was
surprised that a Jewish man would talk to a
Samaritan woman. I like Jesus. (That's good, isn't

it?) He never lets rules or old traditions get in the way. You need something to drink. He's going to bring you some water, no matter who rolls their eyes.

Has there been a time when Jesus came to you in an unexpected way or place? Tell that story.

"Sir," the woman said, "You have nothing to draw with and the well is deep. Where can You get this living water? Are You greater than our father Jacob, who gave us the well and drank from it himself, as did also his sons and his livestock?"

> Jesus answered, "Everyone who drinks this water will be thirsty again, but whoever drinks the water I give them will never thirst. Indeed, the water I give them will become in them a spring of water welling up to eternal life." (John 4:11-14)

She brought up a valid point: "It's a deep well and you don't have a bucket." I don't know about you, but the first thing that usually comes to my mind when Jesus is trying to do something great for me is why this won't work. "But the doctors said this was incurable." "My kids have been gone so long." "My husband could never change." Jesus said, "I'm gonna' bless your socks off," and she responded, "We've never done it that way before." What do you think God could do for you today if you would just get out of the way?

Let's be really honest for a minute. What is that one thing that you have just about given up on? What have you decided that God can't or won't fix? Confess that now.

The woman said to Him, "Sir, give me this water so that I won't get thirsty and have to keep coming here to draw water."

He told her, "Go, call your husband and come back."

"I have no husband," she replied.

Jesus said to her, "You are right when you say you have no husband. The fact is, you have had five husbands, and the man you now have is not your husband. What you have just said is quite true." (John 4:15-18)

BOOM! Wow! I didn't see that coming. She said, "Okay, I'll have a sip." Jesus said, "Go get your husband and we will finish this talk." She said, "Don't have one." Jesus said, "You've had a bunch." Now, the time of day makes sense. We understand that this lady came to the well in the middle of the day to stay away from everybody else in town. She lived with the shame of who she was and what she had done. If she came in the morning or evening when all the other women came, they would point their fingers at her, they would whisper, not too quietly, and they would call her names like slut, home wrecker, big fat loser.

Shame. Ever been there? (Yes, we are back on shame again. But this is important.) Sitting in church while the preacher preached on some sin and you were wondering how many people were thinking about you. Afraid to go to the store because you might run in to someone who knew your story, and though they would be polite, you would see the condemnation in their eyes. Ever been overwhelmed with your shame? And yet Jesus goes right there.

Why do you think Jesus brought up her past?

She was curious, now.

> "Sir," the woman said, "I can see that You are a prophet. Our ancestors worshiped on this mountain, but you Jews claim that the place where we must worship is in Jerusalem."

"Woman," Jesus replied, "believe me, a time is coming when you will worship the Father neither on this mountain nor in Jerusalem. You Samaritans worship what you do not know; we worship what we do know, for salvation is from the Jews. Yet a time is coming and has now come when the true worshipers will worship the Father in the Spirit and in truth, for they are the kind of worshippers the Father seeks. God is spirit, and His worshippers must worship in the Spirit and in truth."

The woman said, "I know that Messiah (called Christ) is coming. When He comes, He will explain everything to us."

Then Jesus declared, "I, the one speaking to you—I am He." (John 4:19-26)

Oh, there's a good trick. He said, "I'll give you water and you will never thirst again." She said, "Just a sip." He confronted her shame. She then turned the subject to religion. "The Baptists believe once saved always saved. The Methodists don't. Which group is right?" Actually, she said, "We worship in the hills. The Jews worship in Jerusalem. What about that?" That's where we go. "The Pentecostals speak in tongues. The Lutherans don't." "Do you think Jesus is coming back before the tribulation or after?" As soon as the conversation gets a little too personal, as soon as somebody starts stepping on our toes, we turn all high and mighty on them and start talking about doctrine and theological positions. We get religious instead of getting honest. We try to be correct instead of being changed.

There is a huge difference between being Christian and being religious. Most of us are pretty good at being religious. Religion provides a nice little mask to cover our shame. (Yes, we are still on shame.)

Has there ever been a time when you let your "religious" face cover the shame you were dealing with? Talk about that.

Look at the story again. She got religious, but Jesus didn't back down. She started talking church. Jesus said, "I am the Christ." When we finally quit wearing the mask, playing the game, skirting the issues, Jesus will show Himself to us plain and simple. So often in the New Testament, He did *not* tell people who He was. So often He warned them not to tell anyone else.

Why do you think Jesus told this woman, of all people, "I am He?"

Look at the rest of her story:

> Just then his disciples returned and were surprised to find him talking with a woman. But no one asked, "What do you want?" or "Why are you talking with her?"

71

Then, leaving her water jar, the woman went back to the town and said to the people, "Come, see a man who told me everything I ever did. Could this be the Messiah?" They came out of the town and made their way toward him." (John 4:27-30)

Tell about a time when Jesus lovingly pointed his finger at you. We used to call that "being under conviction."

Conclusion

Here's the thing. Jesus doesn't waltz around our sin. He gets right to the point: "Go call your husband." But He does it with such a tender heart, with so much love for us, that instead of condemnation, we feel acceptance. Instead of judgment, we feel compassion. Our story becomes, not something we are trying to hide, but the wonderful testimony of how God loved us when it felt that no one else did.

The woman was so excited she forgot all about water and the well and her bucket. You know we women are excited if we forget about our buckets. She went back to the village and said, "Come see a man who told me everything I've ever done" (John 4:39). She came to the well in the hottest part of the day so that people would not talk about what she had done, and now she's reminding everybody about it. The next thing you know she will be writing a book, *Failure and How I Achieved It*, or something like that. (If you don't recognize the title of my brother's first book you should be ashamed. Just kidding—but order it today.)

> Many of the Samaritans from that town believed in Him because of the woman's testimony, "He told me everything I ever did." So when the Samaritans came to Him, they urged Him to

stay with them, and He stayed two days. And because of His words many more became believers.

They said to the woman, "We no longer believe just because of what you said; now we have heard for ourselves, and we know that this man really is the Savior of the world." (John 4:39-42)

Now, we are making the transition from overcoming shame to being unashamed. When God changes our lives, when He strips away our pretense and religious posturing, we cannot help but speak the Truth boldly. It doesn't matter who we were before. We've got to tell somebody.

The story winds down. People were saved. The disciples were confused. The woman was blessed, and Jesus was satisfied that He was doing His Father's work. And for over 2000 years we have been telling the story of this wonderful woman at the well. That's the way you get rid of shame, right there.

What have you been hiding? What are you so afraid that someone is going to find out? What do you carry around that makes you feel less than or not good enough? The 12 Steps says, "We confessed the nature of our disease to God and to someone we trusted." The 12-Step people say, "Every time we tell our story, our shame is cut in half."

Listen, God loves you and wants to take every bit of shame and embarrassment away from you. He wants you to be free from that junk. He has a heart big enough to stuff all your stuff in. Let Him have it. You have nothing to prove and nothing to hide. And you might be surprised at how many people need to hear your story.

Week 4: Group Time

Prayer: Begin your group time with prayer. Pray that you will see Jesus plainly in your meeting tonight.

Connection: There is a great conversation in Chonda's interview with the Benham brothers about speaking the truth boldly but lovingly. Watch together the Bible study clip for chapter 4 found in the special features of the *Unashamed* DVD.

Centering: Read John 14:7-26 as a script, one person reading only the words of Jesus and one person reading only the words of the woman.

Discussion: Together, go over some of your answers from this week's study. Make sure everyone has a chance to speak about the questions that were most meaningful to them.

Activity: Write together a four-sentence response (no more) to the question, "Why are you a Christian?"

Community: If the group feels comfortable with this, pick a new prayer partner for this week and talk together briefly about prayer needs. Commit to pray for your prayer partner this week.

Closing: Pray that God will give each of you opportunities to tell your story. Set the time and place for next week's meeting.

Notes

Week 5: Becoming a World Changer
Personal Study: Acts 9 and Romans 1:16

We are in week five, nearly finished with our six-week study on being *unashamed*. We spent a little while looking at shame and learning to let God take that from us. Last week we turned the corner and discovered that when God takes our shame away, it can help us to be *unashamed*, to proclaim boldly what Christ has done in us. This week our study will continue in that direction with a different look.

In each interview in the movie *Unashamed*, I was impressed with the fact that these people were willing to stand up for their faith even at the risk of personal loss or sacrifice. The Benham brothers lost a huge TV show, Danny Gokey got booted off of American Idol—all for standing up for what they believed. But in every case, the power to take such a stand came from a profoundly personal, life-changing encounter with Jesus. Let's look at one of those encounters in the Bible.

> As he neared Damascus on his journey, suddenly a light from heaven flashed around him. He fell to the ground and heard a voice say to him, "Saul, Saul, why do you persecute Me?"
>
> "Who are You, Lord?" Saul asked.
>
> "I am Jesus, whom you are persecuting," He replied. "Now get up and go into the city, and you will be told what you must do."
>
> The men traveling with Saul stood there speechless; they heard the sound but did not see anyone. Saul got up from the ground, but when he opened his eyes, he could see nothing. So they led him by the hand into Damascus. For three days he was blind and did not eat or drink anything." (Acts 9:3-9)

You know the story. There was this guy named Saul. He was a nut. He was out to get the Christians and doing everything in his power to destroy this fledgling faith. Sometimes, we complain about being persecuted for our faith. We ain't seen nuthin'! This guy, Saul, was putting people to death for speaking the name of Jesus. But one day, on his way to Damascus First Church, Saul had a knock-you-off-you-horse confrontation with God.

There are five actions that move us from being shame wearers to being unashamed world changers. Here's the first:

Action # 1: Have an encounter with God. It all begins there.

Luke describes what happened to Paul (we're going to talk about that name change later) on the road to Damascus. Blinding light. Loud voice. Falling on the ground. Shoot, he's describing every Sunday at some Pentecostal churches! I don't know exactly what that looks like for you—it's different for all of us—but I do know that you will never reach your full potential until you have a face-to-face, personal, intimate encounter with God.

Let me give you five steps from Paul's Damascus story to help with that.

- **STOP:** Take some time to quiet yourself before God.
- **ASK:** Ask God to speak to you. Go ahead, ask Him.
- **LISTEN:** Respond to the Spirit. What did God say?
- **WAIT:** Be persistent. Sometimes we are so "busy" it takes a minute.

- **LET GOD:** Just let God do whatever He chooses to do in you!

Let's do that right now. What is God trying to say to you?

The story didn't stop on the road to Damascus. God connected Saul with someone to help him grow.

In Damascus there was a disciple named Ananias. The Lord called to him in a vision, "Ananias!"

"Yes, Lord," he answered.

The Lord told him, "Go to the house of Judas on Straight Street and ask for a man from Tarsus named Saul, for he is praying. In a vision he has seen a man named Ananias come and place his hands on him to restore his sight."

"Lord," Ananias answered, "I have heard many reports about this man and all the harm he has done to your holy people in Jerusalem. And he has come here with authority from the chief priests to arrest all who call on your name."

But the Lord said to Ananias, "Go! This man is my chosen instrument to proclaim my name to the Gentiles and their kings and to the people of Israel. I will show him how much he must suffer for my name."

Then Ananias went to the house and entered it. Placing his hands on Saul, he said, "Brother Saul, the Lord—Jesus, who appeared to you on the road as you were coming here—has sent me so that you may see again and be filled with the Holy Spirit." Immediately, something like scales fell from Saul's eyes, and he could see again. He got up and was baptized, and after taking some food, he regained his strength." (Acts 9:10-19)

Action # 2: Become a disciple.

One of the interesting parts of the story of Paul's life is that everyone was afraid of him. He came to faith in Christ. He tried to join the church, but frankly they were scared. Well, he had been going around killing Christians. It would be like Osama Bin Laden all of a sudden showing up and wanting to sing in the choir. God told this Ananias guy to go help Paul, and he said, "No way, God. He is a bad dude." But he went, and Saul/Paul (I know, it's confusing) got his sight back, got baptized, went to a potluck dinner (gotta' love those Baptists), and started to learn about the faith.

Later, "When he came to Jerusalem, he tried to join the disciples, but they were all afraid of him, not believing that he really was a disciple. But Barnabas took him and brought him to the apostles" (Acts 9:26-27). So this one guy, Barnabas, stepped up to Paul and took him under his wing and began to disciple him even though everyone else still had their doubts.

We often try to do this thing on our own. Being truly *unashamed* is hard work. We need somebody or somebodies that we can lean on, learn from, find strength in. Find someone that you respect and ask them to meet with you once a month. When you meet, ask them three questions:

- What should I be reading?
- How should I be praying?
- Where should I be changing?

Have you ever been in a real discipling relationship? If so, why? If not, why not?

Here's the next step.

Action # 3: Focus on getting ready!

Listen, it takes me three hours to get fixed up enough to go out on a date. (Yes, I'm doing that now. Just mind your own business.) But if I want to go out and change the world tomorrow, there's some stuff I need to get better at. There are some answers I don't have yet. I will never know it all, but before I go off half-cocked, I want to spend some time with my mentor and get myself ready. The last half of verse 19 just says, "Saul spent many days in Damascus." In Galatians 1:17 Paul tells us that he went away to Arabia before he started his ministry. Most Bible historians believe that he was gone between 8 and 14 years. At the very least, we should take a little time every day to get away and think about changing our world. Jesus got away early in the morning. Plan, prepare, participate. Take the time to get ready to change the world.

Write the names of five people that God lays on your heart to meet with on a regular basis. Here's a hint. They might be in this Bible study with you right now.

1.

2.

3.

4.

5.

Pray about it, then approach them and see if they would meet with you regularly to get ready to change your world unashamedly.

Action # 4: Learn to pray.

Paul prayed. One of the best stories of his praying is in Acts 16:25. Paul was in jail in Philippi for preaching the Gospel. The Bible said, "About midnight he and Silas were praying and singing songs to God." (If you want to know how that worked out, you can read the story for yourself, but can you say *jailbreak*?) I have never known a genuine world changer, anyone who was truly *unashamed*, who did not really know how to pray. Jesus prayed. Paul prayed. Peter prayed. Everybody who has ever taken a strong stand for Christ prays.

One of my favorite prayer outlines is the Lord's Prayer.

- Hallowed be Thy Name—PRAISE
- Thy Kingdom come—SURRENDER
- Give us this day—PROVISION
- Forgive our debts—CONFESSION
- Lead us not—PROTECTION
- Deliver us from evil—PURITY
- For Thine is the Kingdom—PRAISE

Confession time. On a scale of 1 to 10, how is your prayer life? What do you need to do to make it better?

The next action is closely akin to Action # 4.

Action # 5: Study the Word of God! No, I mean really study it.

In 2 Timothy, Paul told his young disciple, "All Scripture is God-breathed and is useful for teaching, rebuking, correcting and training in righteousness, so that the servant of God may be thoroughly equipped for every good work" (2 Tim. 3:16-17).

Okay, here's the name change deal. When Saul was on the road to Damascus, he was called Saul. When

Ananias went to see him, he was called Brother Saul. When he was preaching on the Greek island of Cyprus, he was called Paul for the first time (Acts 13:9). It seems to me that after his conversion, when he really started changing the world, he got a new name. When you start standing up and being *unashamed*, you can be sure you will get a new name.

That is why we need to make sure we are living in the Book, studying our Bibles daily. Before we can go tall, we had better go deep.

Why do you think Bible study will be so important to you in your bold walk with Jesus?

Now, the last action.

Action #6: Become a discipler! Remember Step 2, become a disciple? Now we start to give what we have been getting.

Paul took all of the lessons he learned from Barnabas and began pouring them into other people: Silas, John Mark, Philemon, Timothy, who is maybe the best known. I challenge you to make a new young-believer friend this year and begin meeting with this person once or twice a month for coffee or lunch. Give them a Bible verse to read and then ask these three simple questions:

1. What does this verse say? (Have them say it in their own words.)
2. What does this verse mean??
3. How will you live it out this week?

Listen, if you were going to be *unashamed*, where would you begin? Family, friends, people you work with or go to school with? Start there.

Pray with me right now. "Lord, give me the name of someone that you want me to take under my wing. Open the door for that to happen. Make me unashamed in approaching them about growing together in You." Simple question. **Who? Who did God say to you and what is your plan to begin to disciple this person?**

Conclusion

Remember when we started this chapter, I gave you two passages of scripture? The first is Acts 9, which is the conversion story of Saul; we looked at that pretty well.

The other is Romans 1:16. Here's what it says. (It's Paul speaking, by the way.) "I am not ashamed of the Gospel, because it is the power of God for the salvation of everyone who believes, first for the Jew and then for the Gentile." Wow! How cool is that? Paul must have seen my movie. Saul, the persecutor of the church, had a life-changing encounter with Jesus. He got discipled. He focused on getting ready. He learned to pray. He studied the Word of God. He took other people under his wing. At some point, he stood up tall, shook his fist in the face of all of those who were calling him names, and posted on his FaceBook page, "I AM NOT ASHAMED OF THE GOSPEL." What a change! All that he cared about was introducing people to the One who changed him.

Which leads to one more action, **Action #7:** Share your faith!

Here is a simple little plan based on the acronym SALT.

- SAY something good.
- ASK questions.
- LISTEN.
- TURN the conversation to Christ.

We can do this. We may not be world changers. We may have a pretty small circle of influence and don't imagine that what we do counts for a whole lot. But you know what, it matters to somebody. And it sure matters to Jesus.

Week 5: Group Time

Prayer: Begin your group time with prayer. Begin praying for boldness to share your story and to reach someone for Christ.

Connection: Watch the clip together from the movie where the Benham brothers talk about being persecuted for their faith. The Bible study clip for chapter 5 is found in the special features of the *Unashamed* DVD. Watch that together and talk about it.

Centering: Read Acts 9:1-31. Have each person in the group read a few verses.

Discussion: Together, go over some of your answers from this week's study. Make sure everyone has a chance to speak about the questions that were most meaningful to them.

Activity: Put a chair in the middle of the room. One at a time, have each member of the group sit in it while the rest pray for that person. End the prayer for each person with this paraphrase of Romans 1:16: Call them by name and say, "*You* are not ashamed of the Gospel."

Community: If the group feels comfortable with this, pick a new prayer partner for this week and talk together briefly about prayer needs. Commit to pray for your prayer partner this week.

Closing: Pray that God will give each one of you a person to disciple. Set the time and place for next week's meeting.

Week 6: God Chooses Who He Uses
Personal Study: Luke 7:36-50

Can you believe we are here already? This is the beginning of the last week of our six weeks together. It has flown by. We have talked about *shame* and how Jesus so wants to take that away from us. We have talked about *unashamed* and how Jesus so wants us to be that. Here we are in week six and we will connect the two things one more time. It is the very fact that He has removed our *shame* that gives us the power to be *unashamed*. And it is found in one of my favorite stories. Turn with me to Luke 7.

> When one of the Pharisees invited Jesus to have dinner with him, He went to the Pharisee's house and reclined at the table. A woman in that

93

town who lived a sinful life learned that Jesus was eating at the Pharisee's house, so she came there with an alabaster jar of perfume. As she stood behind Him at His feet weeping, she began to wet His feet with her tears. Then she wiped them with her hair, kissed them and poured perfume on them.

When the Pharisee who had invited Him saw this, he said to himself, "If this man were a prophet, He would know who is touching Him and what kind of woman she is—that she is a sinner." Jesus answered him, "Simon, I have something to tell you." "Tell me, teacher," he said.

"Two people owed money to a certain money lender. One owed him five hundred denarii, and the other fifty. Neither of them had the money to pay him back, so he forgave the debts of both. Now which of them will love him more?"

Simon replied, "I suppose the one who had the bigger debt forgiven." "You have judged correctly," Jesus said. Then He turned toward the woman and said to Simon, "Do you see this woman? I came into your house. You did not give me any water for My feet, but she wet My feet with her tears and wiped them with her hair. You did not give Me a kiss, but this woman, from the time I entered, has not stopped kissing My feet. You did not put oil on My head, but she has poured perfume on My feet. Therefore, I tell you, her many sins have been forgiven—as her great love has shown. But whoever has been forgiven little loves little." Then Jesus said to her, "Your sins are forgiven."

The other guests began to say among themselves, "Who is this who even forgives sins?" Jesus said to the woman, "Your faith has saved you; go in peace." (Luke 7:36-50)

This is the longest story we have read so far, but this is only a piece of a much longer story. We have to do a quick bit of Bible research. This woman didn't have a name in this story, so who was she? Did she ever show up again? Did she become a true Christ follower?

Well, a woman much like her showed up early in Jesus's ministry in John chapter 8. She was the woman taken in adultery. Remember that story? The religious snobs threw her at Jesus's feet and said, "She needs to be put to death."

Jesus didn't say anything, just stooped down and started writing in the dirt, probably a list of all of their hypocritical sins.

They slipped away, *ashamed*. He asked the woman, "Where are your accusers?" She said, "Ain't nobody." And Jesus said, "Then I sure won't condemn you. Go and sin no more."

Shortly after this event was the story of the "sinful" woman who was so appreciative of what Jesus had done for her that she poured her best Chanel No. 5 on His feet and wiped it off with her hair, as Luke told. Coincidence? Most Bible scholars think this was the same woman, the one from John 8. In the very next chapter, Luke 8, a new follower of Jesus is introduced, Mary from Magdala, Mary Magdalene. Man, this is getting good.

Last piece. In John 12, the story of Jesus raising Lazarus from the dead has just wrapped up. He had two sisters we are all familiar with, Martha and, you guessed it, Mary. Now, in chapter 12 Jesus was having supper at their house. In John 12:3, John said, "Then Mary took about a pint of pure nard, an expensive perfume; she poured it on Jesus's feet and wiped His feet with her hair." The woman who was forgiven of adultery was the woman who anointed Jesus's feet, and that was the Mary of the famous Mary, Martha, and Lazarus trio. So cool.

This woman who had so much to be ashamed of had become such a close and intimate follower of

Jesus that she washed His feet, even when it ticked off the old religious fuddy duddies.

Here are some good questions. When is the last time you washed Jesus's feet? **What do you do on a regular basis to just express your deep gratitude for Him and worship of Him? How could you do that better?**

I want you to know that this call to live *unashamed* is not all that complicated. We try to figure it out, fix it up, create a mission statement, organize a ministry team, prepare the presentation, develop an objective—I'm exhausted before I ever start. It's not that hard. First, God chooses who He uses.

Think of all the people who came in contact with Jesus. Imagine all of those that Jesus could have chosen to tell about things like grace, devotion, surrender, courage, commitment, and loyalty. Of all the people that Jesus could have singled out, He picked this very suspect woman to become one of the heroes of the faith.

God chose me when I was most un-choosable. I could write a book about all of my failures and faults. (Oh, I did.) Of all the people in the world that I would choose to be used by God, I would not be one of them. But He chose me in spite of me.

By the way, He chooses you. The same John who tells us about this woman writes in another place, "To him who loves us and has freed us from our sins by his blood, and has made us to be a kingdom and priests to serve his God and Father —to Him be glory and power for ever and ever! Amen" (Rev. 1:6).

What does it mean to you that Jesus has chosen you?

Paul says, "For it is by grace you have been saved, through faith—and this is not from yourselves, it is the gift of God—not by works, so that no one can boast. For we are God's handiwork, created in Christ Jesus to do good works, which God prepared in advance for us to do" (Eph. 2:8-10).

The first and most basic step in finding your ministry is recognizing that it will find you. God has chosen you. He created you. He called you. He has given you a purpose. One phrase in John 8:32 stands out: "and the truth will set you free."

How does telling the truth about your own story set you free from shame?

The second thing is that God uses who He chooses. He chooses who He uses, and He uses who He chooses. Can I be honest? I probably wouldn't have picked you. That's okay. I wouldn't have picked me, either. What do you think she felt when old Simon the Pharisee said, "Lord, this woman is a sinner?" Her face turned crimson. She dropped her head. And Jesus said, "Let me tell you something, Simey old boy. I have chosen this woman and I am going to use her because of her heart of gratitude."

What do you think about that? She didn't deserve to be chosen by God. Surely, she wasn't fit for ministry. Neither was David, or Samson, or Moses, or Peter, or Paul, or me, or you. But God uses who He chooses. He tells a parable about the thankfulness that comes and our response to His grace. Listen, if she had been Mother Teresa, that story would have made no sense. It was her very past that allowed God to use her in such a magnificent way. He commended her for doing what no one else had done. God chooses who He uses and uses who He chooses.

What in your story makes you think God could *not* use you right now? This is important: Write your answer in pencil.

Read again the ending to this story:

> Then He turned toward the woman and said to Simon, "Do you see this woman? I came into your house. You did not give Me any water for My feet, but she wet My feet with her tears and wiped them with her hair. You did not give Me a kiss, but this woman, from the time I entered, has not stopped kissing My feet. You did not put oil on My head, but she has poured perfume on My feet. Therefore, I tell you, her many sins have been forgiven—as her great love has shown. But whoever has been forgiven little loves little." Then Jesus said to her, "Your sins are forgiven." The other guests began to say among themselves, "Who is this who even forgives sins?" Jesus said to the woman, "Your faith has saved you; go in peace." (Luke 7:44-50)

Write one more time about that wonderful moment of forgiveness for you. Where were you? How old were you? What was going on?

Put your testimony down on paper so that you can rejoice over it again.

Here's one final point. God chooses who He uses. God uses who He chooses. And only God can bless our mess. There is nothing that you have done, no place that you have gone, no sin that you have committed that puts you in a place where God can't reach you or won't forgive you. Where does our boldness come from? What gives us the courage to be *unashamed*? It is the amazing forgiveness of God. Remember, He had already forgiven Mary in the street when the hypocritical religious guys had thrown her at His feet. But now, just to make sure there was no doubt and just to make sure it was publicly known, He said again, "I forgive you." In fact, He said it twice, once talking to Simon about her and then directly to her. It is as if Jesus was saying, "Look, all you people who are passing judgment, for the rest of history, this woman and the forgiveness I have given her will be talked about." What a blessing!

Right now, ask God to tell you what blessing He has for you in spite of your mess-ups. Write that down.
_____

Conclusion

Our call is to live *unashamed*. The way we do that is by having the absolute assurance that that He has "forgiven us of *all* our sins and cleansed us from *all* unrighteousness" (1 John 1:9).

Let's do one last piece of Bible research. Fast forward to the end of Jesus's earthly story. In In his gospel, John is telling the story of the Crucifixion. He says, "Near the cross of Jesus stood His mother, His mother's sister, Mary the wife of Clopas, and Mary Magdalene" (John 19:25). Most of His followers had fled. Peter had denied Him. All the big, bad boys had gone. There was left to be named just three or four women, and one of them was Mary.

Three days passed. "Early on the first day of the week, while it was still dark, Mary Magdalene went to the tomb and saw the stone had been removed from the entrance" (John 20:1). Now, I know the other Gospel writers expanded this story a bit and included some other women, but in all accounts, Mary Magdalene was there. In John's account, she was the only one. From a very shameful encounter in the middle of the road, Mary had been a devoted follower of Christ for the rest of His ministry. She loved Him and worshipped Him even when others thought she should not. She stood at the Cross when most had left. And John used her to be the first to know that He was no longer in the grave. How awesome is that! This woman was *unashamed*.

That's all that this is about. We are so thankful, so grateful for what He has done that we refuse to leave His side, even when the world makes it hard for us. We do not back down. We do not give up. We do not lose heart. We are forgiven. We are *unashamed*.

Week 6: Group Time

Prayer: Begin your group time with prayer. Begin praying for boldness to share your story and to reach someone for Christ.

Connection: This week's Bible study clip for chapter 6 is found in the special features of the *Unashamed* DVD. Watch that together and talk about it.

Centering: Read Luke 7:36-50. Have each person in the group read a few verses.

Discussion: Together, go over some of your answers from this week's study. Make sure everyone has a chance to speak about the questions that were most meaningful to them.

Activity: Want to be really brave? Get a large bowl of water, a few towels, and wash one another's feet, declaring the love of God for them as you do. Now, go back in your book to the answer you wrote in pencil this week to this question: "What in your story makes you think God could not use you right now?" *Erase your answer!*

Community: If the group feels comfortable with this, pick a new prayer partner for this week and talk together briefly about prayer needs. Commit to pray for your prayer partner this week.

Closing: Pray together that God will lead you to the next steps of living *unashamed*.

Information

For help with depression, addiction, or family counseling, contact:

Branches Counseling Center

Phone: (615) 904-7170

BranchesCounselingCenter.com

For more information for Chonda Pierce go to

www.chonda.org

If you'd like to read more of Mike's writing, go to

www.branchesblog.com.

Notes